Natasha Alexandrova

Workbook 1

Russian Step By Step for Children

Editors: Ellen Weaver, Anna Watt

Illustrations: Elena Litnevskaya, Irka Verbol

Cover: Natalia Illarionova

russianstepbystepforchildren.com

Second Edition

Russian Step By Step for Children

Workbook 1

All rights reserved

Copyright © 2014 by Russian Step By Step

No part of this book may be reproduced or transmitted in any form or by any means: electronic or mechanical, including photocopying, recording, or by any information storage and retrieval system, without written permission from the publisher.

ISBN-13: 978-1500817268

ISBN-10: 1500817260

Printed in the United States of America

Наташа Александрова

Книга студента 1

Русский шаг за шагом для детей

Редакторы: Елена Вивер, Анна Вотт

Иллюстрации Елены Литневской

Обложка Натальи Илларионовой

russianstepbystepforchildren.com

Contents

COURSE COMPONENTS 8
   Free Audio Component 9
   Structure of the Workook 1 10

PRIMARY COURSE 13

RUSSIAN ALPHABET 14

LESSON 1 15
   Буквы А, К, М, О, С, Т, П, Л 15
   Это маска. Буква Э 17
   Да. Буква Д 17
   Нет. Буквы З, Е, Н 18

LESSON 2 20
   Буквы Б, И, Ч. Кто это? Что это? 20
   Или 21
   Буква Ф 23

LESSON 3 25
   Буквы В, Г. Что это такое? 25
   Буквы Я, Р. Я, он, она, они 27
   Это, то 28

LESSON 4 32
   Буквы Ж, У 32
   А или И? Тоже 32
   Буква Ё 33

Буква Й. Это мой чай. 34

LESSON 5 37

Буквы Х, Ц 37

Буквы Ъ, Ь. Он, она, оно 39

Где? 40

LESSON 6 43

Буквы Ш, Щ 43

Буква Ы. Я, вы, мы. 45

Буква Ю 46

Посчитаем! 0 – 10 48

GRAMMAR AND TRANSLATION 49

Russian Alphabet 50

LESSON 1 51

Greetings 51

Reading Russian 51

Verb 'to Be' 51

Unstressed O 52

Intonation 52

Is This …?/Translation 52

LESSON 2 54

Who is this? What is this?/Translation 54

Is This Tom or Linda?/Translation 54

LESSON 3 56

What Is This?/Translation 56

Personal Pronouns: я, он, она, они 56

   This/That 57
LESSON 4 58
   Conjunctions: а, и 58
   This Is My Brohter/Translation 58
   Names 59
LESSON 5 60
   Silent Letters: ь, ъ 60
   Gender of Nouns 60
   Where …?/Translation 61
LESSON 6 62
   Personal Pronouns: ты, вы, and мы 62
   I Am Olya/Translation 62
   Counting 0 -10 63
ANSWER KEY 64
GRAMMAR TABLES 68
   Personal Pronouns 69
   Numbers 69
DICTIONARIES 70
   Russian-English Dictionary 71
   English-Russian Dictionary 76

Course Components

Welcome to the Russian Step By Step Learning System!

Russian Step By Step for Children *Workbook 1* is the first step in this series.

This course includes a **Workbook** and the corresponding **Audio** (Direct Download from a website).

Each audio track is indicated by a loud speaker and a number: 🔊 **2** . That is the track number you need to listen to. The track numbers and the exercise numbers do not match. Please download the digital file to your computer, electronic player, phone or record it to a CD.

We recommend that you listen to all the audio tracks, even if some of the exercises were covered in class. Please listen to the past lessons, as that helps with retention. Listen to the audio in the car (especially during the long trips), while walking, or working out – the more you can incorporate the audio tracks into your everyday activities, the more you will improve your *retention, comprehension, and pronunciation*.

FREE Audio Component

By purchasing this book, you receive the **FREE audio** component right away!

To access the complimentary **Direct Digital Audio Download** please:

- Go to RussianStepByStepChildren.com/Registration   Make sure you are on the correct website, as there is a Russian Step By Step Series for Adults (It has a different website).

- Create your username and password

- After registration you will receive an email to verify your email address. Press the verification link, and **you are ready to listen!**

- Download the audio Tracks on your computer through the top menu: Books>RSBS for Children>Audio Download

- If you have any questions, please email us at info@russianstepbystep.com

Structure of the Workbook 1

The *Workbook 1* has four parts: Primary Course, Grammar, Answer Key, and Dictionaries.

The ***Primary Course*** section consists of 6 lessons. Each lesson introduces new words and new grammar that are practiced in the exercises.

The ***Grammar*** section corresponds to the 6 lessons in the Primary Course. Here you will find the explanation of new language and grammar rules that will help you use this language properly. In this section you will also find translation of the new vocabulary.

The ***Answer Key*** section provides the answers for the exercises.

The ***Dictionaries***: Adjectives are given in their masculine form. Words are given with the definitions that are used in this book.

Dear Adults!

Our Series *Russian Step By Step for Children* consists of many steps. Every book is another step that brings engaging and successful lessons of the Russian Language to the children.

This Series is designed for the children in elementary and middle school (8 - 14 years old).

For children in preschool and kindergarten – please use our series *Azbuka*.

For the children in high school, college students and adults – please use our series *Russian Step By Step School Edition.*

This series is a step-by-step introduction to the Russian language for children who do not speak Russian or have a limited exposure to the Russian language. Depending on the level of the child, you can begin using any step of this series.

Our series consists of a *Workbook*, *Audio* (Direct Download for a website), a *Teacher's Manual, Slides, and Games*. If you are a parent or a relative of the child and will be leading the lessons, you will require the *Teacher's Manual*. If you are a teacher - we promise that the *Teacher's Manual* will greatly facilitate your lesson plan preparation and significantly cut your lesson prep time.

Upon completion of this book the student will be able to read in Russian, will learn how to form positive and negative statements, yes/no questions, general (who, what, where) questions, you will learn about genders of Russian nouns, you will also learn Personal Pronouns (я, ты, он, она, оно, мы, вы, они) and counting 0 – 10.

For the parents and relatives of the children who will use the book:

Please read the instructions on how to work with this book. You will be the biggest helper to the child outside of the classroom, even if you do not know any Russian.

    1. At the end of the book you will find the grammar explanations and translations. You do not have to cover them, but if the child expresses interest or asks you about some details they talked in class, this part will help you give the correct answers.

    2. Use the audio at home not only as part of the homework assignments, but also to cement the covered material. Listen not only to the last lesson, but to at least three preceding lessons. It will help remember the previously covered material.

    3. The *Workbook* contains a certain specifically selected amount of material that the student needs. The main outline of the lesson is located in the Teacher's Manual. If you use this to study by yourself, please start from the Teacher's Manual.

    4. Cover all the exercises in the lesson first orally and then in writing. It would be good to assign the exercises as written homework, after you have covered them orally in class. This repeated use helps to reinforce the new material.

    5. The guiding principle of this book is that the children do not need to be presented with a large volume of new information (grammar, vocabulary). It is more important to work and play with the material

presented in each lesson, until the student feels comfortable with it. So do not rush – high speed of presentation and a large volume of new material only make the lesson harder for the children. If you want to add something to the lesson – use the additional components of this series (games, handouts, slides) that cover the same vocabulary and grammar.

Primary Course

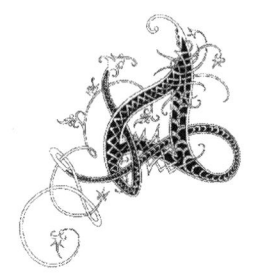

Russian Alphabet

🔊 | 1 |

А а	*Аа*	Б б	*Бб*	В в	*Вв*	Г г	*Гг*
Д д	*Дд*	Е е	*Ее*	Ё ё	*Ёё*	Ж ж	*Жж*
З з	*Зз*	И и	*Ии*	Й й	*Йй*	К к	*Кк*
Л л	*Лл*	М м	*Мм*	Н н	*Нн*	О о	*Оо*
П п	*Пп*	Р р	*Рр*	С с	*Сс*	Т т	*Тт*
У у	*Уу*	Ф ф	*Фф*	Х х	*Хх*	Ц ц	*Цц*
Ч ч	*Чч*	Ш ш	*Шш*	Щ щ	*Щщ*	ъ	*ъ*
ы	*ы*	ь	*ь*	Э э	*Ээ*	Ю ю	*Юю*
Я я	*Яя*						

Lesson 1

А а, К к, М м, О о, С с, Т т, П п, Л л

Exercise 1

Read the following words, then listen to the audio and repeat after the native speaker. After that, write the words down.

1. па́па _____

2. ма́ма _____

3. кот _____

4. стол _____

5. ла́мпа _____

6. сала́т _____

7. сок _____

8. ка́ска _____

Э

Это ма́ска.   Это молоко́.

4

$$это = [эта]$$

Exercise 2

5

Create statements, following the example. Listen to the audio and repeat.

1. __Это мама.__

2. _____

3. _____

4. _____

5. _____

6. _____

16

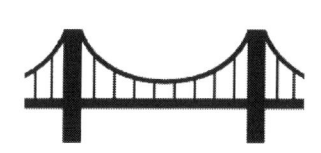

Д

- Э́то дом?
- Да, э́то дом.

- Э́то мост?
- Да, э́то мост.

Exercise 3

Create pairs of questions and answers about the following pictures, as in the example.

1. __Э́то па́па? Да, э́то па́па.__

2. _____

3. _____

4. _____

5. _____

6. _____

З, Е, Н 🔊 7

- Это молоко?
- Нет, это не молоко. Это нота.

- Это мост?
- Нет, это не мост. Это знак «Стоп».

Exercise 4

Answer the questions, following the example.

1. Это сок? __**Нет, это не сок. Это маска.**__

2. Это молоко? _____

3. Это дом? _____

4. Это кот? _____

5. Это салат? _____

6. Это знак «Стоп»? _____

7. Это ла́мпа? _____

8. Это ма́ска? _____

Exercise 5 - тест

1. _____
2. _____
3. _____
4. _____
5. _____
6. _____
7. _____
8. _____
9. _____

Lesson 2

Б, И, Ч

- Э́то чемпио́н.

- Э́то кот?
- Нет, это не кот.
- Кто это?
- Это соба́ка.

- Это ма́ска?
- Нет, это не маска.
- Что это?
- Это диск.

Exercise 6

Create a question for each statement, as in the example.

1. Это мама. __**Кто это?**__

2. Это мост. _____

3. Это па́па. _____

4. Это знак «Стоп». _____

5. Это сала́т. _____

6. Это пило́т. _____

7. Это молоко. _____

8. Это А́нна. _____

9. Это ка́ска. _____

Или 🔊 9

- Это Том и́ли Ли́нда?
- Это Линда.

- Это пчела́ и́ли соба́ка?
- Это пчела́.

Exercise 7 🔊 10

Answer 'or' questions, following the example.

1. Это кот или соба́ка? __**Это кот.**_____

2. Это ма́ска или знак «Стоп»? _____

3. Это но́та или чек? _____

4. Это дом или стадио́н? _____

5. Это бана́н или лимо́н? _____

6. Это банк или такси́? _____

Exercise 8   🔊 11

Read the following words, then listen to the audio and repeat after the native speaker. Consult the dictionary, if you are not sure about the meaning. Write the words down.

1. лимона́д **лимонад**_____ 2. бале́т _____

3. анекдо́т _____ 4. систе́ма _____

5. чемпио́н _____ 6. мета́лл _____

7. дипло́м _____ 8. капита́н _____

9. поли́тика _____ 10. домино́ _____

| ф | Это фо́то. | Это фен. | - Это кака́о?
- Это не кака́о. Это ко́фе. | 12 |

Exercise 9　　13

Answer the questions, following the example.

1.  Это ма́ска? **Это не маска. Это диск.**

2.  Это мост? _____

3.  Это о́фис? _____

4. Это бана́н? _____

5. Это дипло́м? _____

6. Это соба́ка? _____

Exercise 10 - тест

1. _____
2. _____
3. _____
4. _____
5. _____
6. _____
7. _____
8. _____
9. _____

Lesson 3

В, Г

Что это такое?

🔊 14

- Кто это?

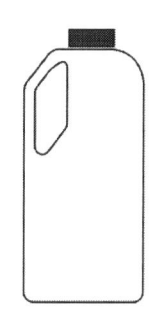

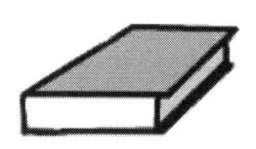

Это человéк.

- Это молоко или водá?

- Это молоко.

- А что это такóе?

- Это книга́.

Что это? = Что это такое?

Exercise 11

Ask questions about animate (living beings) and inanimate objects and answer them, following the example.

1. **Что это такое? Это банан.**

2. **Кто это? Это человек.**

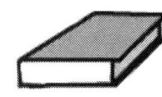

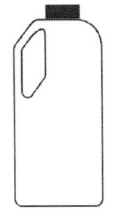

3. _____

4. _____

5. _____

6. _____

7. _____

8. _____

9. _____

10. _____

Я   # Я Оля   🔊 15

Я Оля.    Он Ива́н.    Она́ Светла́на.    Они́ Анто́н и Ни́на.

Р   # Это балерина или доктор?   🔊 16

- Это балери́на или до́ктор?
- Это балери́на.

- Это крокоди́л или зе́бра?
- Это зе́бра.

Exercise 12

Read the following words, then listen to the audio and repeat after the native speaker. Consult the dictionary if you need help with translation. Write the words down.

1. метро́ **метро**
2. фи́рма _____
3. спортсме́н _____
4. актри́са _____
5. Ро́берт _____
6. со́ус _____
7. Мари́я _____
8. па́спорт _____
9. дире́ктор _____
10. класс _____
11. бизнесме́н _____
12. Аме́рика _____
13. рестора́н _____
14. Калифо́рния _____
15. торт _____
16. Аргенти́на _____

Это/то

Э́то я́блоко.
То мандари́н.

- Что э́то?   - Э́то очки́.
- Что то?   - То стака́н.

Exercise 13

Create pairs of questions and answers about near and distant objects.

1. **Кто то? То кот.**

   Кто это? Это пчела.

2. _____

   _____

3. _____

   _____

4. _____

   _____

5. _____

   _____

6. _____

   _____

29

Exercise 14

Answer the questions, following the example.

1. Это до́ктор? **Нет, это не доктор. Это балерина.**

2. Это зе́бра? _____

3. Это я́блоко? _____

4. Это стака́н? _____

5. Это ко́фе? _____

6. Это пчела́? _____

Exercise 15 - тест

1. _____
2. _____
3. _____
4. _____
5. _____
6. _____
7. _____
8. _____
9. _____
10. _____

_____

Lesson 4

Ж, У   **А или И?**   🔊 19

Это муж, а это жена́.   Ж-ж-ж-ж....

Это жук, и это то́же жук.

Exercise 16

Write statements about the following pictures using the proper conjunctions **а** or **и**.

1. __**Это нота, а это маска.**__

2. __**Это кот, и это тоже кот.**__

3. _____

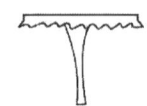

4. _____

5. _____

6. _____

7. _____

8. _____

9. _____

Это пилот, а то самолёт

Ё

ёж ёлка Это пилот, а то самолёт.

Exercise 17

🔊 **21**

Read the following words, then listen to the audio and repeat after the native speaker. Consult the dictionary if you need help with translation. Write the words down.

1. бокс **бокс**   2. ро́бот _____

3. платфо́рма _____   4. актёр _____

5. сувени́р _____   6. пинг-понг _____

7. парк _____   8. футбо́л _____

9. зоопа́рк _____   10. гимна́стика _____

11. сигна́л _____   12. гара́ж _____

13. лимона́д _____   14. жира́ф _____

й

Это мой чай

🔊 **22**

Это мой брат.   Это мой чай.   Это мой стул.

Никола́й, Андре́й, Алексе́й, Григо́рий, Матве́й.

🔊 **23**

Exercise 18

Pretend that all of the following objects are yours. Write statements about them.

1. _____Это мой дом._____
2. _____
3. _____
4. _____
5. _____
6. _____
7. _____

Exercise 19

🔊 **24**

Usually all foreign names should sound similar to their origin. Listen to the audio, repeat after the native speaker, and try to write the following names in Russian.

1. **Джон** _____
2. _____
3. _____
4. _____
5. _____
6. _____
7. _____
8. _____

9. _____   10. _____

11. _____   12. _____

13. _____   14. _____

15. _____   16. _____

17. _____   18. _____

19. _____   20. _____

Exercise 20 - тест

1. _____

2. _____

3. _____

4. _____

5. _____

6. _____

7. _____

8. _____

9. _____

10. _____

11. _____

Lesson 5

X, Ц   **Холодно!**   🔊 25

хлеб 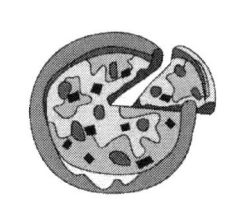   пи́цца    Хо́лодно!

Exercise 21   🔊 26

Read the following words, then listen to the audio and repeat after the native speaker. Consult the dictionary if you need help with translation. Write the words down.

1. кио́ск **киоск**   2. хокке́й *а* _____

3. аэропо́рт _____   4. лимузи́н _____

5. бадминто́н _____   6. информа́ция _____

7. ре́гби _____   8. ко́бра _____

9. ко́смос _____   10. музе́й _____

11. поли́ция _____   12. суп _____

Exercise 22

Answer the questions, following the example.

1. Это ресторан? **Нет, это не ресторан. Это кафе.**

2. Это жук? _____

3. Это хлеб? _____

4. Это очки? _____

5. Это авокадо? _____

6. Это киоск? _____

7. Это крокодил? _____

Это семья

ь, ъ

ь   Это семья́.   Это жильё.

1) семья́   жильё
2) мать   контро́ль   конь

ъ въезд   объём   подъём

Он, она, оно

Он: стол, музе́й, конь - **согласная, ь**

Она: мама, А́нглия, ёлка, мать – а, я, ь

Оно: кафе́, я́блоко – о, е

Папа - он

Где?

- Где пу́дель?
- Вот он.

- Где меда́ль?
- Вот она́.

- Где окно́?
- Вот оно́.

Exercise 23

Divide the following words into three columns according to the gender.

Ма́ма, па́па, челове́к, ва́за, ко́фе, кни́га, мета́лл, окно́, пчела́, соба́ка, чемпио́н, Григо́рий, я́блоко, семья́, балери́на, кафе́, такси́, контро́ль, меда́ль, метро́, музе́й, авока́до, те́ннис, фо́то, зе́бра, меню́.

он	она	оно
	мама	

Exercise 24

Write pairs of questions and answers about the following pictures, as in the example.

1. __**Где крокодил? Вот он.**__
2. _____
3. _____
4. _____
5. _____
6. _____
7. _____
8. _____
9. _____
10. _____
11. _____
12. _____
13. _____
14. _____

Exercise 25 - тест

1. _____
2. _____
3. _____
4. _____
5. _____
6. _____
7. _____
8. _____
9. _____
   _____
10. _____

Lesson 6

Ш, щ   **Это бабушка**   🔊 30

Это бабушка.   Это дедушка.   Это шоколад.

борщ   вещь   щенок

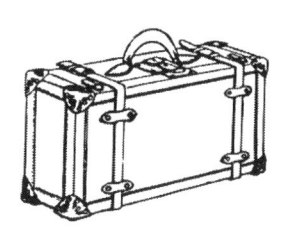

🔊 31

Exercise 26

Read the following words, then listen to the audio and repeat after the native speaker. Consult the dictionary if you need help with translation. Write the words down.

1. Чика́го **Чикаго** _____

2. Вашингто́н _____

3. центр _____

4. шокола́д _____

5. пингви́н _____ 6. щено́к _____

7. шо́рты _____ 8. секрета́рша _____

9. диало́г _____ 10. теа́тр _____

11. Ната́ша _____ 12. ма́фия _____

Exercise 27

Create short dialogues, following the example.

1. Это ёлка? **Это ёлка? Нет, это не ёлка.**
   Кто это? Это жира́ф.

2. Это шокола́д? _____

3. Это щено́к? _____

4. Это пу́дель? _____

5. Это вещь? _____

6. 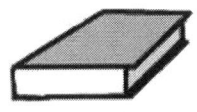 Это борщ? _____

_____

7.  Это музе́й? _____

_____

Ы - И   32

Ы

мы – ми   вы – ви   ры - ри   ны – ни   ты – ти

33

Я О́ля.   Ты Ива́н.   Вы Светла́на.   Мы Ни́на и Анто́н.

рыба   цветы   сыр   🔊 34

Ю

Нью-Йорк   Юлия   Юрий   🔊 35

🔊 36

Exercise 28

Read the following words, then listen to the audio and repeat after the native speaker. Consult the dictionary if you need help with translation. Write the words down.

1. Нью-Джéрси **Нью-Джерси**
2. гиппопотáм _____
3. журнáл _____
4. минúстр _____
5. мýзыка _____
6. джúнсы _____
7. визúт _____
8. спорт _____
9. мирáж _____
10. инструмéнт _____
11. саксофóн _____
12. фрукт _____
13. туалéт _____
14. клуб _____

46

Exercise 29

Answer the following questions, as in the example.

1. Это пчела? __**Нет, это не пчела. Это пудель.**__

2. Это цветы? _____

3. Это хлеб? _____

4. Это бабушка? _____

5. Это ёлка? _____

6. Это стул? _____

7. Это борщ? _____

Посчита́ем! 0 - 10

🔊 37

0 – ноль   1 – оди́н   2 – два   3 – три

4 – четы́ре   5 – пять   6 – шесть   7 – семь

8 – во́семь   9 – де́вять   10 – де́сять

Exercise 30 - тест

1. _____
2. _____
3. _____
4. _____
5. _____
6. _____
7. _____
8. _____
9. _____
10. _____

Grammar and Translation

Russian Alphabet

Despite the fact that the Cyrillic alphabet looks different from the Roman one, it is pretty easy to learn.

In the Russian alphabet, as in many others, letters have names and corresponding sounds.

Reading in Russian is really easy compared to English. There are certain rules for reading, and if you know them, you can read any word.

For example, in English it is impossible for a foreigner to read the words bl**oo**d, p**oo**r, and fl**oo**r correctly if he/she does not know that the pronunciation of **oo** varies. This does not happen in Russian.

Therefore, to be able to read Russian, you have to learn the sounds that the Russian letters make and the pronunciation rules.

Read the alphabet once, trying to understand how the letters are pronounced. Concentrate on the sounds (see the transliteration column).

Some of the letters are really easy, because they look very similar to English ones and make similar sounds: А, О, Т, Е, К, and С.

Some of the letters look different, but make sounds found in English: Б, Г, Д, Ё, Ч, Ж, И.

Some of the letters look different from English letters and are pronounced differently from any English sounds: Щ, Ы, Ц.

And some of them look similar to English letters but make different sounds: Р, Н, В, Х.

Those are the tricky ones, but everything comes with practice.

All Russian words in Russian Step By Step books are given with a stress mark. Knowing which vowel is stressed in the word is very important because it affects pronunciation.

There are 33 letters in the Russian alphabet: 10 vowels, 21 consonants, and two letters which do not make any sounds by themselves. These are called the hard sign and the soft sign. You will learn about these two letters in Lesson 5.

Lesson 1

Greetings

Dear student, you don't know the Russian alphabet yet, but you can learn the greeting by heart without seeing it written. Listen to the Track2 and repeat after the native speaker.

Reading Russian

Reading Russian is much easier than it might look, which means that most of the time you pronounce all the letters in each word.

А а, К к, М м, О о, С с, Т т   These six letters look similar and make the sounds similar to English ones.

    A like **a** in f**a**ther   **K** like **k** in **k**itten   **M** like **M** in **m**an

    O like **o** in s**o**rt   **C** like **c** in **c**eiling   **T** like **t** in **t**oy

П п, Л л   These two letters look different from but sound similar to English letters:

    П like English **P** in **p**et   **Л** like **L** in **l**amp

Articles

There are no articles in the Russian language.

    кот = *a cat or the cat*

Verb 'To Be'

In most cases, the verb **to be** is not used in the Present Tense.

Это маска. = *This is a mask.* (Literally: This mask.)

Это салат. = *This is a salad.*

Э The letter **э** is pronounced like **e** in b**e**d.

Unstressed 'O'

Pay attention to the pronunciation of the letter **o** in the word **это**. The letter **o** is pronounced like **a** when not stressed.

это = [эта]

Intonation

Questions are formed using a rising intonation. The word order is the same in affirmative and interrogative sentences.

Это дом? = *Is this a house?*

Да, это дом. = *Yes, this is a house.*

Д The letter **д** is pronounced like **d** in **d**og.

З The letter **з** is pronounced like z in **z**ebra.

Е The letter **E** looks like the English **E**. However, it is pronounced like **ye** in **ye**t.

Н The letter **Н** is a tricky one, because it looks like an English letter **h**, but it is pronounced like **n** in **n**o.

The good thing about this letter is that you will memorize it easily, because it stands for Russian **нет** (no). Therefore, you will use it a lot.

Is This... ?/Translation

Это молоко? = *Is this milk?*

Нет, это не молоко. Это нота. = *No, this is not milk. This is a note.*

Это мост? = *Is this a bridge?*

Нет, это не мост. Это знак «Стоп». = *No, this is not a bridge. This is a Stop sign.*

In the first six lessons, the last exercise is a comprehension test. It's supposed to be done in class with your teacher.

Lesson 2

И, Б, Ч   These three letters look different but make sounds that exist in English:

Б like **b** in **b**oy   **И** like **ee** in w**ee**k   **Ч** like **ch** in **ch**ange

Who Is This? What Is This? /Translation

Это чемпион. = *This is a champion.*

Это кот? = *Is this a cat?*

Нет, это не кот. = *No, this is not a cat.*

Кто это? = *Who is this?*

Это собака. = *This is a dog.*

Это маска? = *Is this a mask?*

Нет, это не маска. = *No, this is not a mask.*

Что это? Это диск. = *What is this? This is a disk.*

Notice that the letter **ч** in the word **что** is pronounced like **sh** in **sh**eep. This is an exception.

что = [што]

Is This Tom or Linda?/Translation

Это Том или Линда? = *Is this Tom or Linda?*

Это Линда. = *This is Linda.*

Это пчела или собака? = *Is this a bee or a dog?*

Это пчела. = *It is a bee.*

Ф The letter **ф** is pronounced like **f** in **f**ather.

    Это фото. = *This is a photo.*

    Это фен. = *This is a fan.*

    Это какао? = *Is this cocoa?*

    Это не какао. Это кофе. = *It's not cocoa. It's coffee.*

Lesson 3

В, Г The Russian letter **В** can be confused with the English letter **b**, but it is pronounced like **v** in **v**an.

The letter **Г** looks different from any English letter, but is pronounced like **g** in **g**ame.

What Is This? /Translation

Кто это? = *Who is this?*

Это человек. = *This is a person.*

Это молоко или вода? = *Is this milk or water?*

Это молоко. = *It is milk.*

А что это такое? = *And what is this?*

Это книга. = *This is a book.*

Что это? = Что это такое? = *What is this?*

These two questions are both translated into English the same way. The word **такое** just adds more curiosity.

Personal Pronouns: я, он, она, они

Я The letter **Я** is pronounced like **ya** in **ya**rd.

Let's learn four Personal Pronouns.

я = *I*   он = *he*   она = *she*   они = *they*

Я Оля. = *I am Olya.*

Он Иван. = *He is Ivan.*

Она Светлана. = *She is Svetlana.*

Они Антон и Нина. = *They are Anton and Nina.*

As you see, the structure of the sentences above is very simple. It was already mentioned in the first lesson that the verb **to be** usually omitted in the Present Tense.

Р The letter **Р** can be challenging at the beginning, because there is no equivalent sound in English for it. The closest sound to the Russian letter **Р** is **r** in **r**un. But of course it's not the same. Just listen to the native speaker and repeat it many times. Don't worry if you don't reproduce it correctly. Everything comes with practice.

    Это балерина или доктор? = *Is this a ballerina or a doctor?*

    Это балерина. = *This is a ballerina.*

    Это крокодил или зебра? = *Is this a crocodile or a zebra?*

    Это зебра. = *It's a zebra.*

This/That/Translation

There are two words in Russian that replace the phrases 'this is' and 'that is'.

For near objects, we use the word **это**. For distant objects, we should use the word **то**.

    это = *this is = these are*   **то** = *that is = those are*

    Это яблоко. = *This is an apple.*

    То мандарин. = *That is a tangerine.*

    Что это? = *What is this?*

    Это очки. = *These are glasses.*

    Что то? = *What is that?*

    То стакан. = *That is a glass.*

As you see, we use **это/то** for both singular and plural in the Present Tense.

Lesson 4

Ж, У The letter **Ж** looks unfamiliar to an English speaker, but is pronounced like **su** in trea**su**re.

The letter **у** looks like English **y** but is pronounced like **oo** in m**oo**d.

Conjunctions: а, и

There are two Russian conjunctions - **а** and **и** - that can be translated into English as the conjunction **and**.

>Это муж, а это жена. = *This is a husband and this is a wife.*

>Это жук, и это тоже жук. = *This is a beetle and this is also a beetle.*

Notice how the conjunctions **а** and **и** join the sentences.

When we talk about two different things, we use **а**.

When we talk about two similar things, we use **и**.

Ё The letter **Ё** is pronounced like **you** in **you**r. It is not difficult to memorize **Ё**, because this is the only letter that has two dots above it. The letter **Ё** is always stressed.

Й The letter **Й** is pronounced like **y** in bo**y**.

This Is My Brother/Translation

The Russian word **мой** means **my**.

>Это мой брат. = *This is my brother.*

>Это мой чай. = *This is my tea.*

>Это мой стул. = *This is my chair.*

Names

Many Russian male names have **й** at the end.

    Николай, Андрей, Алексей, Григорий, Матвей.

Spelling of English names in Russian needs to be practiced, too. There is no letter corresponding to the English letter J, therefore in Russian we have to use two letters instead of **J** (дж).

    John = Джон   James = Джеймс   Julia = Джулия

Most of the time, in a foreign name the Russian letter **e** is pronounced like э.

    Kevin = Кевин (Кэвин)   Margaret = Маргарет (Маргарэт)

Lesson 5

Х, Ц — The letter **Х** is another tricky one. It looks like English X but is pronounced similar to **h** in **h**at.

The letter **Ц** looks different from any English letter but is pronounced exactly like **ts** in boo**ts**.

    Холодно! = *It's cold!*   пицца = *pizza*   полиция = *police*

Silent Letters

ь, ъ — These two letters are silent letters.

ь – the soft sign has two main functions:

    1) it works as a separation sign when it is followed by a vowel

        семья = family   жильё = housing

    2) it softens the preceding consonant

        мать = *mother*   контро́ль = *control*   конь = *horse*

In order to feel the difference, the soft sign makes, listen to the audio and repeat after the native speaker.

ъ – the hard sign works as a separation sign in the same way as the soft sign does. (In ancient times **ъ** was used a lot, but now it is used very rarely. There are not that many words with the hard sign.)

        въезд = *entrance* (for cars)   объём = *volume*   подъём = *ascent*

Gender of Nouns

All Russian nouns can be divided into three groups, according to their gender: masculine, feminine, and neuter. In the majority of cases, you can tell the gender of the word by its ending.

Nouns that end in the soft sign can be either masculine or feminine. In this case, you can find out the gender from the dictionary.

- он: сто**л**, музе**й**, кон**ь** — masculine nouns end in a consonant or in a soft sign

- она: Англи**я**, ёлк**а**, мат**ь** — feminine nouns end in **a** or **я** or in a soft sign

- оно: каф**е**, яблок**о** — neuter nouns end in **o** or **e**

And of course there are exceptions:

папа is a masculine word.

Let's learn a new phrase, in which we should remember a gender of a noun.

Where …?/Translation

Где пудель? = *Where is the poodle?*

Вот он. = *Here it is.*

Где медаль? = *Where is the medal?*

Вот она. = *Here it is.*

Где окно? = *Where is the window?*

Вот оно[1]. = *Here it is.*

The pronouns **он** and **она** are used for both **living beings** and **inanimate objects**.

The pronoun **оно** is used only **for inanimate objects.**

---

[1] Оно is a Personal Pronoun that is used for the neuter objects.

Lesson 6

Ш, Щ   The letter **Ш** is pronounced as **sh** in **sh**awl.

    Это бабушка = *This is a grandma.*

    Это дедушка. = *This is a grandpa.*

The letter **Щ** looks similar to Ш, but has a little leg and is pronounced softer, as **shsh** in Engli**sh sh**ip.

    борщ = *Russian beet (beetroot) soup*   вещь = *thing*   щенок = *puppy*

Ы   The letter **Ы** is pronounced similar to **i** in s**i**t. The letter **Ы** is often confused with **И**. Listen to the pairs of syllables with different consonants and compare the sounds. (Audio Track 33)

Ю   The letter **Ю** is pronounced like **you** in **you**.

    Юрий   Юлия

Personal Pronouns: ты, вы, мы

In Lesson 3 we learned four Personal Pronouns. Let's learn three more.

    ты = *you* (informal)   вы = *you (polite)*   мы = *we*

There are two forms of addressing people in Russian: formal (or polite) - **вы** and informal - **ты**. The general rule is:

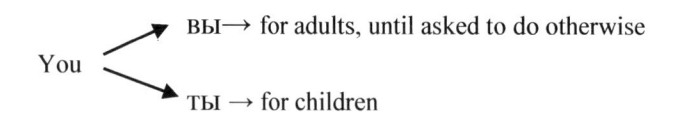

    You   → вы → for adults, until asked to do otherwise
           ↘ ты → for children

I Am Olya/Translation

    Я Оля. = *I am Olya.*

    Ты Иван. = *You are Ivan.*

Вы Светлана. = *I am Svetlana.*

Мы Антон и Нина. = *We are Anton and Nina.*

Counting 0 - 10

Посчитаем! = *Let's count!*

In order to memorize the numbers faster, try to count everything around you in Russian.

Answer Key

Exercise 3

2. Это лампа? Да, это лампа. 3. Это стол? Да, это стол. 4. Это маска? Да, это маска. 5. Это салат? Да, это салат. 6. Это молоко? Да, это молоко.

Exercise 4

2. Нет, это не молоко. Это лампа. 3. Нет, это не дом. Это стол. 4. Нет, это не кот. Это дом. 5. Нет, это не салат. Это мост. 6. Нет, это не знак «Стоп». Это молоко. 7. Нет, это не лампа. Это нота. 8. Нет, это не маска. Это знак «Стоп».

Exercise 6

2. Что это? 3. Кто это? 4. Что это? 5. Что это? 6. Кто это? 7. Что это? 8. Кто это? 9. Что это?

Exercise 7

2. Это знак «Стоп». 3. Это нота. 4. Это дом. 5. Это банан. 6. Это такси.

Exercise 9

2. Это не мост. Это фен. 3. Это не офис. Это дом. 4. Это не банан. Это лимон. 5. Это не диплом. Это фото. 6. Это не собака. Это пчела.

Exercise 11

3. Что это такое? Это лимон. 4. Кто это? Это пчела. 5. Что это такое? Это кофе. 6. Что это такое? Это книга. 7. Что это такое? Это молоко. 8. Кто это? Это собака. 9. Что это такое? Это фото. 10. Что это такое? Это ваза.

Exercise 13

2. Что то? То лимон. Что это? Это яблоко. 3. Что то? То молоко. Что это? Это вода. 4. Что то? То книга. Что это? Это очки. 5. Что то? То кофе. Что это? Это фото. 6. Кто то? То собака. 6. Кто это? Это зебра.

Exercise 14

2. Нет, это не зебра. Это пчела.   3. Нет, это не яблоко. Это мандарин.   4. Нет, это не стакан. Это торт.   5. Нет, это не кофе. Это сок.   6. Нет, это не пчела. Это человек.

Exercise 16

3. Это стол, и это тоже стол.   4. Это лимон, а это банан.   5. Это ваза, и это тоже ваза. 6. Это торт, а это каска.   7. Это пчела, а это жук.   8. Это лампа, и это тоже лампа. 9. Это человек, а это собака.

Exercise 18

2. Это мой крокодил.   3. Это мой мандарин.   4. Это мой стакан.   5. Это мой ёж. 6. Это мой чай.   7. Это мой сок.

Exercise 19

1. Джон;   2. Джоан;   3. Джимми;   4. Джулия;   5. Боб;   6. Нэнси;   7. Фрэнк;   8. Дебора; 9. Кевин;   10. Мэри;   11. Майк;   12. Лаура;   13. Грэг;   14. Дженнифер;   15. Джо; 16. Патрисия;   7. Ричард;   18. Барбара;   19. Джейсон;   20. Маргарет.

Exercise 22

2. Нет, это не жук. Это ёж.   3. Нет, это не хлеб. Это яблоко.   4. Нет, это не очки. Это ёлка.   5. Нет, это не авокадо. Это пицца.   6. Нет, это не киоск. Это стул. 7. Нет, это не крокодил. Это жираф.

Exercise 23

Он: папа, человек, кофе, металл, чемпион, Григорий, контроль, музей, теннис.

Она: мама, ваза, книга, пчела, собака, семья, балерина, медаль, зебра.

Оно: окно, яблоко, кафе, такси, метро, авокадо, фото, меню.

Exercise 24

2. Где мандарин? Вот он.　3. Где кофе? Вот он.　4. Где хлеб? Вот он.　5. Где пицца? Вот она.　6. Где такси? Вот оно.　7. Где стул? Вот он.　8. Где чай? Вот он.　9. Где кафе? Вот оно.　10. Где ёж? Вот он.　11. Где ёлка? Вот она.　12. Где яблоко? Вот оно.　13. Где жираф? Вот он.　14. Где зебра? Вот она.

Exercise 27

2. Нет, это не шоколад. Что это? Это медаль.　3. Нет, это не щенок. Кто это? Это ёж.　4. Нет, это не пудель. Что это? Это пицца.　5. Нет, это не вещь. Кто это? Это балерина.　6. Нет, это не борщ. Что это? Это книга.　7. Нет, это не музей. Что это? Это хлеб.

Exercise 29

2. Нет, это не цветы. Это рыба.　3. Нет, это не хлеб. Это сыр.　4. Нет, это не бабушка. Это дедушка.　5. Нет, это не ёлка. Это щенок.　6. Нет, это не стул. Это окно.　7. Нет, это не борщ. Это цветы.

Grammar Tables

Personal Pronouns

I	You Informal	You Polite	We	He	She	It Neuter object	They
я	ты	вы	мы	он	она	оно	они

Numbers

0	1	2	3	4
ноль	один	два	три	четыре
5	6	7	8	9
пять	шесть	семь	восемь	девять
10				
десять				

Dictionaries

Russian - English Dictionary

Every time a noun ends in a soft sign or has an irregular ending for the certain gender it is indicated by:

m - masculine   *f* – feminine   *n* - neuter

А

а and, but, oh, so
абрико́с apricot
авока́до avocado
авто́бус bus
администра́ция administration
а́дрес address
аква́риум aquarium
актёр actor
актри́са actress
алфави́т alphabet
Аме́рика America
анекдо́т anecdote, funny story
А́фрика Africa
аэропо́рт airport

Б

ба́бушка grandmother
бага́ж baggage
бадминто́н badminton
бале́т ballet
балери́на ballerina
балко́н balcony
бана́н banana
банк bank
баскетбо́л basketball
бассе́йн swimming pool
бегемо́т hippopotamus
бизнесме́н businessman
блок block
бокс boxing
борщ beet (beetroot) soup

босс boss
брасле́т bracelet
брат brother
бриз sea breeze
бу́ква letter
бума́га paper

В

ва́за vase
вещь thing
вода́ water
въезд entrance (for vehicles)
вы you (polite *sing/pl*)

Г

гара́ж garage
где where
геогра́фия geography
гео́лог geologist
геро́й hero
гимна́стика gymnastics
гость *m* guest
гру́ппа group

Д

да yes
де́вочка little girl
де́вять nine

де́душка grandfather
десе́рт dessert
де́сять ten
джи́нсы jeans
диало́г dialogue
диза́йнер designer
дипло́м diploma
дире́ктор director
диск disk
до́ктор doctor
докуме́нт document
до́ллар dollar
дом house, building
дочь daughter

Е

ещё still, yet, more

Ё

ёж hedgehog
ёлка fir tree

Ж

жена́ wife
жильё housing, accommodation
жира́ф giraffe
жук beetle
журна́л *n* magazine

З

здра́вствуйте [здраствуйте] Hello
зе́бра zebra
знак sign
зо́на zone
зоопа́рк zoo

И

и and
и́ли or
И́ндия India
инжене́р engineer
информа́ция information
Испа́ния Spain
Ита́лия Italy

К

кака́о cocoa
Калифо́рния California
калькуля́тор calculator
Кана́да Canada
кана́л channel
капита́н captain
кафе́ café
ке́мпинг campsite
кио́ск kiosk
класс classroom, grade
клие́нт client
клуб club
кни́га book
ко́бра cobra
колле́га colleague
ко́лледж college
компа́ния company
компози́тор composer
компью́тер computer
кондиционе́р air conditioner
контро́ль *m* control
конце́рт concert
конь *m* horse
коридо́р bullfight, corridor
ко́смос cosmos, (outer) space
костю́м suit, costume
кот cat
ко́фе *m* coffee

крокоди́л crocodile
кто who

Л

ла́мпа lamp
ли́лия lily
лимо́н lemon
лимона́д lemonade
лимузи́н limo
литерату́ра literature
литр liter

М

майоне́з mayonnaise
ма́льчик little boy
ма́ма mom
мандари́н tangerine
ма́ска mask
масса́ж massage
матема́тика math
мать mother
ма́фия mafia
маши́на car, machine
меда́ль *f* medal
медсестра́ nurse (female)
Ме́ксика Mexico
ме́неджер manager
меню́ menu
мета́лл metal
метро́ metro
микроско́п microscope
мини́стр minister
ми́нус minus
мину́та minute
мира́ж mirage
мой my
молоко́ milk
моме́нт moment
мо́ре sea
муж husband

музе́й museum
му́зыка music
мы we

Н

не not
нет no
ноль *m* zero
но́мер number
нос nose
но́та note
Нью Дже́рси New Jersey
Нью Йорк New York
нюа́нс nuance

О

образе́ц example
объём volume
огуре́ц cucumber
оди́н one
о́зеро lake
окно́ window
он he
она́ she
оно́ it, a neuter object
они́ they
о́пера opera
орке́стр orchestra
Отвеча́йте! Answer!
отли́чно *adv* perfect, excellent
о́фис office
о́чень *adv* very
очки́ glasses, spectacles

П

панора́ма panorama
па́па dad
парк park
парла́мент parliament

пассажи́р passenger
па́спорт passport
пацие́нт [пациэ́нт] patient
пило́т pilot
пи́цца pizza
план plan
платфо́рма platform
плюс plus
Повторя́йте! Repeat!
пожа́луйста [пажа́луста] welcome, please
пока́ bye
поли́тика politics
помидо́р tomato
поня́тно! *adv* I see! It's clear!
посчита́ем [пащита́ем] let's count; let's calculate
президе́нт president
приве́т Hi! (informal)
при́нтер printer
прия́тно *adv* pleasant
пробле́ма problem
программи́ст programmer
прое́кт project
прости́те I am sorry
профе́ссия profession
профе́ссор professor
пу́дель *m* poodle
пчела́ bee
пять five

Р

ра́дио radio
рестора́н restaurant
реце́пт recipe
ро́бот robot
ро́за rose
Росси́я Russia
рубль *m* ruble

ру́сский *adj* Russian
ру́чка pen
ры́ба fish

С

саксофо́н saxophone
сала́т salad
сантиме́тр centimeter
сви́тер sweater
секрета́рша secretary (female)
семья́ family
се́рый gray
сигна́л signal
ско́лько how much, how many
слова́рь *m* dictionary
слон elephant
Слу́шайте! Listen!
снег snow
соба́ка dog
сок juice
со́лнце sun
со́ус sauce
спаси́бо thank you
спорт sport
спортсме́н sportsman, athlete
стадио́н stadium
стака́н glass
станда́рт standard
стол table
стоп *n* stop
студе́нт student
стул chair
сувени́р souvenir
суп soup
сыр cheese

Т

такси́ taxi
теа́тр theater
текст text
телеви́зор TV set

телефо́н phone
те́ннис tennis
тепе́рь *adv* now, nowadays
то́же also
торт cake
трамва́й tram
тра́нспорт transport
три three
тролле́йбус trolleybus
трюк trick
туале́т toilet, restroom
тури́ст tourist
ты you (informal singular)

У

упражне́ние exercise
уро́к lesson

Ф

факс fax
фе́рмер farmer (male)
фи́зика physics
фильм film
фи́рма firm
фо́то photo
фотогра́фия photograph
фра́за phrase
Фра́нция France
фрукт fruit
футбо́л soccer

Х

хлеб bread
хокке́й hockey
хо́лодно *adv* cold
хорошо́ *adv* good, OK, well

Ц

цветы́ flowers
центр center

Ч

чай *n* tea
часы́ *pl* clock, watch
ча́шка cup
чек *n* check
челове́к person
чемпио́н champion
четы́ре four
что [што] what, that

Ш

шесть six
шко́ла school
шокола́д chocolate
шо́рты shorts

Щ

щено́к puppy

Э

эконо́мика economy
э́то this

Ю

юри́ст lawyer

Я

я I
я́блоко *n* apple

English-Russian Dictionary

A

accommodation **жильё**
actor **актёр**
address *n* **а́дрес**
administration **администра́ция**
Africa **А́фрика**
airport **аэропо́рт**
alphabet **алфави́т**
also **то́же**
America **Аме́рика**
and **а, и**
anecdote **анекдо́т**
animal **зверь**
Answer! *v* **Отвеча́йте!**
apple *n* **я́блоко**
apricot **абрико́с**
aquarium **аква́риум**
athlete **спортсме́н**
avocado **авока́до**

B

badminton **бадминто́н**
baggage **бага́ж**
balcony **балко́н**
ballerina **балери́на**
ballet **балет**
banana **бана́н**
bank **банк**
basketball **баскетбо́л**
bee **пчела́**
beetle **жук**
beet (beetroot) soup **борщ**
block **блок**
book **кни́га**

boss **босс**
boxing **бокс**
boy **ма́льчик** (little)
bracelet **брасле́т**
brother **брат**
bus **авто́бус**
businessman **бизнесме́н**
bye **пока́** (informal)

C

café **кафе́**
cake **торт**
calculator **калькуля́тор**
California **Калифо́рния**
camera **фотоаппара́т**
campsite **ке́мпинг**
Canada **Кана́да**
captain **капита́н**
car **маши́на**
cat **кот**
center *n* **центр**
chair **стул**
champion **чемпио́н**
channel **кана́л**
check *n* **чек**
cheese **сыр**
chemistry **хи́мия**
chocolate *n* **шокола́д**
classroom **класс**
classroom **класс**
client **клие́нт**
clock *pl* **часы́**
club **клуб**

cobra ко́бра
cocoa кака́о
code код
coffee *m* ко́фе
cold *adv* хо́лодно
colleague колле́га
college ко́лледж
company компа́ния
computer компью́тер
comrade това́рищ
concert конце́рт
conditioner кондиционе́р
control *m* контро́ль
corridor коридо́р
cosmos ко́смос
costume костю́м, наря́д
crocodile крокоди́л
cucumber огуре́ц
cup ча́шка

D

dad па́па
daughter дочь
day *m* день
designer дизайнер
dialogue диало́г
dictionary *m* слова́рь
diploma дипло́м
director дире́ктор
discotheque дискоте́ка
disk диск
doctor врач
document докуме́нт
dog соба́ка
dollar до́ллар

E

economy эконо́мика
eight во́семь
elephant слон
engineer инженерн

entrance (for vehicles) въезд
example образе́ц
excellent *adv* отли́чно
excuse me извини́те
exercise упражне́ние

F

family семья́
farmer фе́рмер
fax факс
film фильм
firm фи́рма
fir tree ёлка
fish ры́ба
five пять
flowers цветы́
four четы́ре
France Фра́нция
fruit фрукт

G

garage гара́ж
gallery галере́я
giraffe жира́ф
girl де́вочка (little) де́вушка (in her late teens)
glass стака́н
glasses очки́ (spectacles)
good *adv* хорошо́
grade класс
grandfather де́душка
grandmother ба́бушка
group гру́ппа
guest *m* гость

H

he он
hedgehog ёж
Hello! Здра́вствуйте! [здраствуйте]

hero геро́й
hippopotamus бегемо́т
home *n* дом
horse *m* конь
house дом
housing жильё
how как
how much, how many ско́лько
human being челове́к
husband муж

I

I я
if е́сли
India И́ндия
information информа́ция
Internet интерне́т
it (neuter object) оно́
Italy Ита́лия

J

jeans джи́нсы
juice сок

K

kiosk кио́ск

L

lamp ла́мпа, торше́р (floor lamp)
language язы́к
limo лимузи́н
lemon лимо́н
lemonade лимона́д
lesson уро́к
letter бу́ква
lily ли́лия
Listen! *v* Слу́шайте!
liter литр

literature литерату́ра

M

mafia ма́фия
magazine журна́л
manager ме́неджер
mask ма́ска
massage масса́ж
math матема́тика
medal *f* меда́ль
menu меню́
metal мета́лл
metro метро́
Mexico Ме́ксика
microscope микроско́п
milk молоко́
minister мини́стр
minus ми́нус
minute мину́та
mirage мира́ж
mistake оши́бка
mobile моби́льный
mom ма́ма
moment моме́нт
Moscow Москва́
mother мать
motorcycle мотоци́кл
museum музе́й
music му́зыка
my мой

N

New Jersey Нью Дже́рси
New York Нью Йорк
next to ря́дом с
night *f* ночь
nine де́вять
no нет
not не
note но́та

now сейча́с [сичас], тепе́рь
nuance нюа́нс
number но́мер
nurse медсестра́ (female) медбра́т (male)

O

object вещь
office кабине́т, о́фис
Oh! А!
OK *adv* ла́дно, хорошо́
one оди́н
opera о́пера
or и́ли
orange *n* апельси́н
orchestra орке́стр

P

panorama панора́ма
paper бума́га
park парк
Parliament парла́мент
passenger пассажи́р
passport па́спорт
patient пацие́нт [пациэнт]
pen ру́чка
perfect *adv* отли́чно
person челове́к
pharmacy апте́ка
phone телефо́н
photo фо́то
photograph фотогра́фия
phrase фра́за
pilot *n* пило́т
pizza пи́цца
plan план
platform платфо́рма
pleasant *adv* прия́тно
please пожа́луйста [пажалуста]
plus плюс
politics *sing* поли́тика

poodle *m* пу́дель
president президе́нт
printer при́нтер
problem пробле́ма, вопро́с
profession профе́ссия
professor профе́ссор
programmer программи́ст
project прое́кт
puppy щено́к
puree пюре́

Q

question *n* вопро́с

R

radio ра́дио
rain *m* дождь
Repeat! Повторя́йте!
restaurant рестора́н
restroom туале́т
robot ро́бот
rose *n* ро́за
ruble *m* рубль
rugby ре́гби
Russia Росси́я
Russian *adj* ру́сский

S

salad сала́т
sauce со́ус
saxophone саксофо́н
school шко́ла
sea мо́ре
sea breeze бриз
secretary секрета́рь (male), секрета́рша (female)
seven семь
she она́
shorts шо́рты

sign (symbol) *n* знак
sign *v* подпи́сывать
signal сигна́л
sister сестра́
six шесть
snow *n* снег
so а
soccer футбо́л
son сын
soup суп
souvenir сувени́р
Spain Испа́ния
sport спорт
stadium стадио́н
standard станда́рт
stop *n* остано́вка, стоп
student студе́нт
subtitle субти́тр
suit *n* костю́м
sweater сви́тер
system систе́ма

T

table стол
tangerine мандари́н
taxi такси́
ten де́сять
tennis те́ннис
text текст
thank you спаси́бо
theater теа́тр
they они́
thing вещь
this э́то
three три
toilet туале́т
tomato помидо́р
tongue язы́к
tourist тури́ст
tram трамва́й
transport тра́нспорт
trick трюк

trolleybus тролле́йбус
TV set телеви́зор
two два

U

university университе́т

V

vase ва́за
very о́чень
volume объём

W

watch *pl* часы́
water вода́
we мы
welcome пожа́луйста [пажалуста]
well хорошо́
watch *n pl* часы́
where где
wife жена́
who кто
window окно́

Y

yes да
you (polite singular/*pl*) вы

Z

zebra зе́бра
zero *m* ноль
zip code и́ндекс
zone зо́на
zoo зоопа́рк

80

Available Titles

Children's Series: Age 3 - 7

1. Azbuka 1: **Coloring Russian Alphabet:** Азбука- раскраска (Step 1)
2. Azbuka 2: **Playing with Russian Letters:** Занимательная азбука (Step2)
3. Azbuka 3: **Beginning with Syllables:** Мои первые слоги (Step 3)
4. Azbuka 4: **Continuing with Syllables**: Продолжаем изучать слоги (Step 4)
5. **Animal Names and Sounds**: Кто как говорит Part 1
6. **Animal Names and Sounds: Coloring Book:** Кто как говорит Part 2
7. Propisi for Preschoolers 1: **Russian Letters: Trace and Learn:** Тренируем пальчики (Step 1)

Children's Series: Age 8 - 14

1. **Workbook 1:** Reading Russian Step By Step for Children (Book & Audio)
2. **Teacher's Manual 1**: Russian Step By Step for Children
3. **Workbook 2:** Russian Step By Step for Children (Book & Audio)
4. **Teacher's Manual 2:** Russian Step By Step for Children
5. **Workbook 3:** Reading Russian Step By Step for Children (Book & Audio)
6. **Teacher's Manual 3**: Russian Step By Step for Children
7. Russian Handwriting 1: **Propisi 1**
8. Russian Handwriting 2: **Propisi 2**
9. Russian Handwriting 3: **Propisi 3**

Adult Learner's Series:

1. **Student Book 1 Beginner:** Russian Step By Step: School Edition (Book & Audio)
2. **Teacher's Manual 1 Beginner**: Russian Step By Step: School Edition
3. **Student Book 2 Low Intermediate:** Russian Step By Step: School Edition (Book & Audio)
4. **Teacher's Manual 2 Low Intermediate**: Russian Step By Step: School Edition
5. **Student Book Intermediate 3:** Russian Step By Step: School Edition (Book & Audio)
6. **Teacher's Manual 3 Intermediate**: Russian Step By Step: School Edition
7. **Student Book 4 Upper Intermediate:** Russian Step By Step: School Edition (Book & Audio)
8. **Teacher's Manual 4 Upper Intermediate**: Russian Step By Step: School Edition
9. Russian Handwriting 1: **Propisi 1**
10. Russian Handwriting 2: **Propisi 2**
11. Russian Handwriting 3: **Propisi 3**
12. **Verbs of Motion**: Workbook 1
13. **Verbs of Motion**: Workbook 2

Printed in Poland
by Amazon Fulfillment
Poland Sp. z o.o., Wrocław